Making
a
baby

Dial Books for Young Readers
An imprint of Penguin Random House LLC, New York

First published in the United States of America by Dial Books for Young Readers,
an imprint of Penguin Random House LLC, 2021

Text copyright © 2020 by Rachel Greener
Pictures copyright © 2020 by Clare Owen
Originally published in the UK by Nosy Crow Ltd, 2020

With thanks to Sylvie Blaustein, certified nurse-midwife, for her input.

Visit us online at penguinrandomhouse.com.

Library of Congress Cataloging-in-Publication Data is available.

Manufactured in Malaysia
ISBN 9780593324851

1 3 5 7 9 10 8 6 4 2

Text set in Filson Pro

Making a baby

Rachel Greener • Clare Owen

Dial Books for Young Readers

You were a baby once. And so was everyone you know.

In fact, every person who has ever lived started life as a baby.

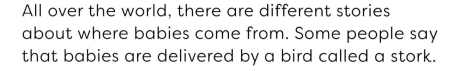

All over the world, there are different stories about where babies come from. Some people say that babies are delivered by a bird called a stork.

Some people say that babies hatch out of eggs like ducks, or crocodiles.

And some people say babies grow in cabbage patches or are found under gooseberry bushes in the garden.

But none of these stories are really true.

Every single baby started life inside at least two different people, and grew inside one person, before being born.

Isn't that amazing?

So how is a baby actually made?

When they are born, most babies are either called boys or girls based on what their bodies look like.

A baby who has a penis and testicles is called a boy. The penis is used for peeing.

Another word for *boy* is *male*.

A baby who has a vulva, which is made up of lots of different parts, is called a girl.

Another word for girl is female.

A tiny hole near the front of the vulva called the urethra is used for peeing.

Behind the urethra is another, bigger hole called the vagina.

But what has this got to do with making a baby?

As people get older, their bodies start to change, so by the time they are a grown-up they can help to make a baby, if they want to.

Testicles are where sperm are made. Sperm are used to help make a baby. Sperm are teeny-tiny and have wriggly tails like tadpoles.

This is what a sperm looks like up close.

This is what a penis looks like inside, and these are testicles.

Breasts can be used to feed milk to a baby.

These are what ovaries look like inside, this is a womb, and this is a vagina.

This is what an egg looks like up close.

Ovaries make eggs. Eggs are used to help make a baby, who grows in a womb.

Every baby starts life as one sperm and one egg. But how do the sperm and egg meet?

**There are lots of ways to make a baby.
One of the ways for a sperm and an egg
to meet is by people having sex.**

Grown-ups have sex in lots of different
ways to show how much they care
about each other, even when they are
not trying to make a baby.

A grown-up with a penis
and a grown-up with a
vagina can make a baby by
having sex, if they want to.

When two grown-ups have
agreed to make a baby
by having sex, they kiss
and cuddle until the penis
becomes hard.

Then they put the penis

inside the vagina.

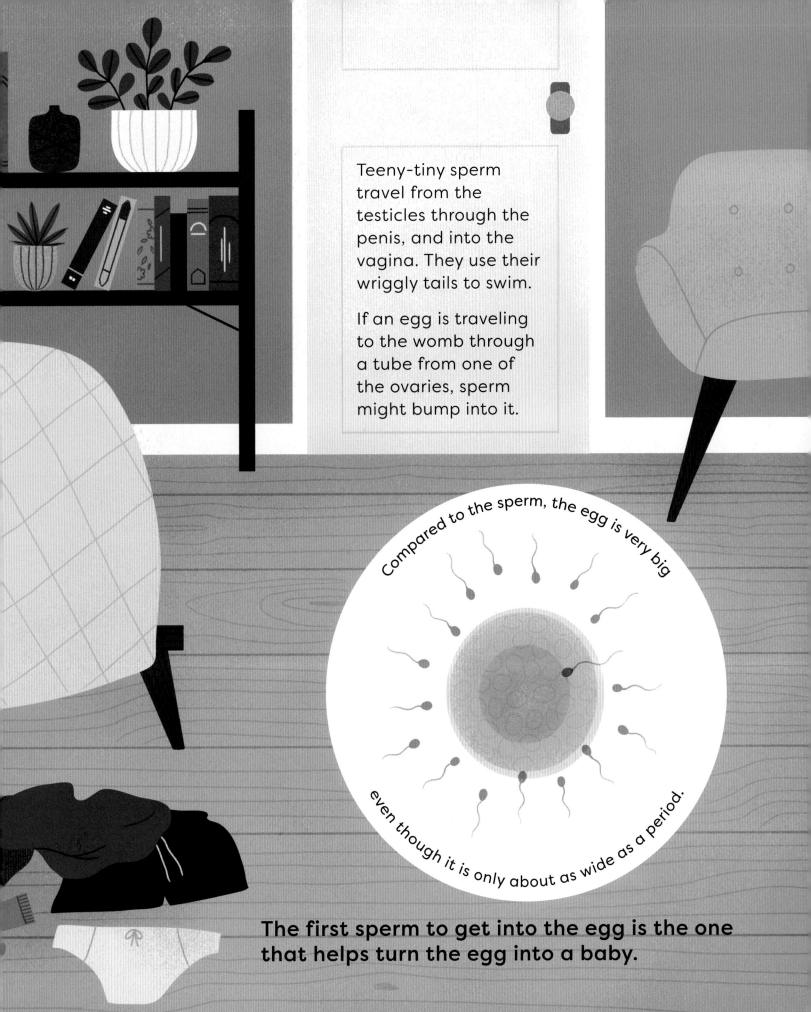

Teeny-tiny sperm travel from the testicles through the penis, and into the vagina. They use their wriggly tails to swim.

If an egg is traveling to the womb through a tube from one of the ovaries, sperm might bump into it.

Compared to the sperm, the egg is very big even though it is only about as wide as a period.

The first sperm to get into the egg is the one that helps turn the egg into a baby.

There are lots of reasons that people who want to have a baby can't—or don't want to—make one by having sex.

Sometimes a person's sperm or eggs might not be working properly. Sometimes a person or couple have eggs but no sperm, or sperm but no eggs, or can't grow a baby inside their body.

One way that scientists can help people to make babies without having sex is by putting sperm directly into the womb of the person who is going to grow the baby.

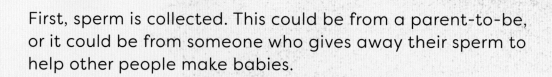

First, sperm is collected. This could be from a parent-to-be, or it could be from someone who gives away their sperm to help other people make babies.

Next, a thin plastic tube is put inside the vagina of the person who will grow the baby.

From there, the sperm travel through the tube and into the womb toward an egg, which will be traveling to the womb through a tube from one of the ovaries.

If the sperm bump into an egg, one of them will help to turn the egg into a baby.

Another way that scientists can help people to make babies is to combine the sperm and the egg in a laboratory.

First, eggs are collected. The eggs could come from the ovaries of a parent-to-be, or they could be from someone who gives away their eggs to help other people make babies.

Next, sperm is collected, either from a parent-to-be, or from someone who gives away their sperm to help other people make babies.

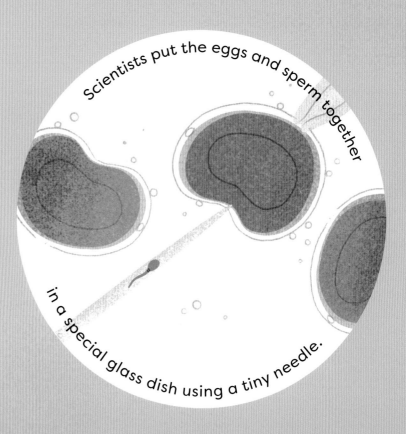

Scientists put the eggs and sperm together in a special glass dish using a tiny needle.

The sperm and egg
join together to make
the very beginning
of a baby, which is
called an embryo.

A doctor then puts the embryo into the womb of
the person who is going to grow the baby.

Families start in all different kinds of ways.

A surrogate grows a baby in their womb for someone who isn't able to do it themselves.

After being born, the baby goes to live with their family.

Sometimes a baby can't be looked after by their birth family, so they are taken care of, or adopted, by a new family instead.

Lots of children all over the world are adopted, sometimes when they are babies and sometimes when they are older.

Being adopted might mean you look different from your parent, or siblings if you have any, but you are loved just as much.

Most babies take around nine months to grow inside the womb. But to begin with, they don't really look like babies at all.

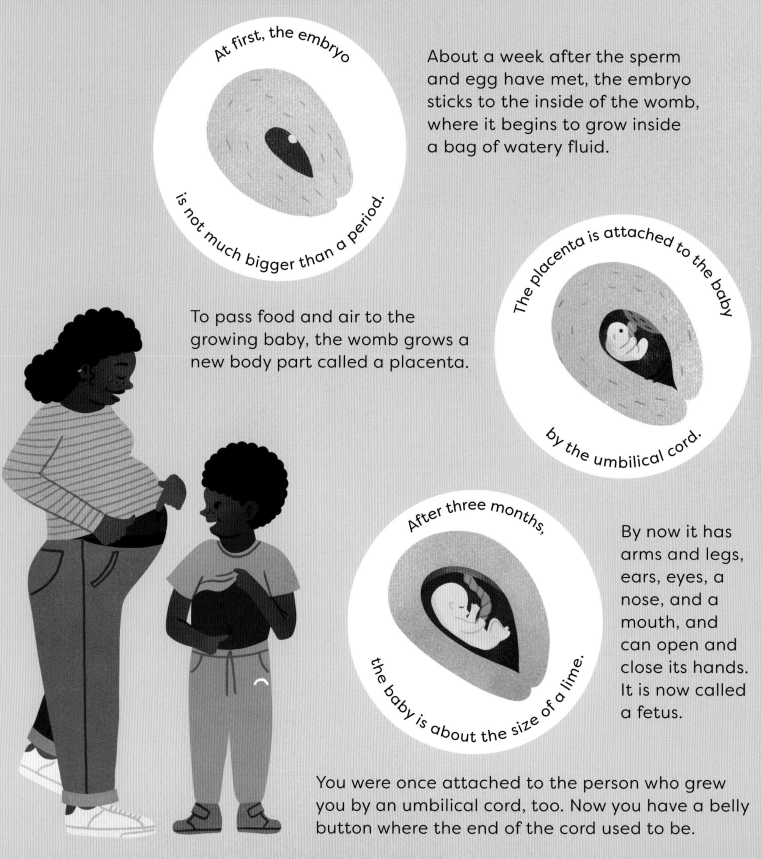

At first, the embryo is not much bigger than a period.

About a week after the sperm and egg have met, the embryo sticks to the inside of the womb, where it begins to grow inside a bag of watery fluid.

To pass food and air to the growing baby, the womb grows a new body part called a placenta.

The placenta is attached to the baby by the umbilical cord.

After three months, the baby is about the size of a lime.

By now it has arms and legs, ears, eyes, a nose, and a mouth, and can open and close its hands. It is now called a fetus.

You were once attached to the person who grew you by an umbilical cord, too. Now you have a belly button where the end of the cord used to be.

Around this time, doctors use a special device, so they can see how the baby is growing inside the womb. This is called an ultrasound machine.

Isn't it amazing to be able to see a baby growing inside a person's womb?!

The fetus can be very wriggly and might even look like it is waving.

Things change quickly as a baby grows inside the womb.

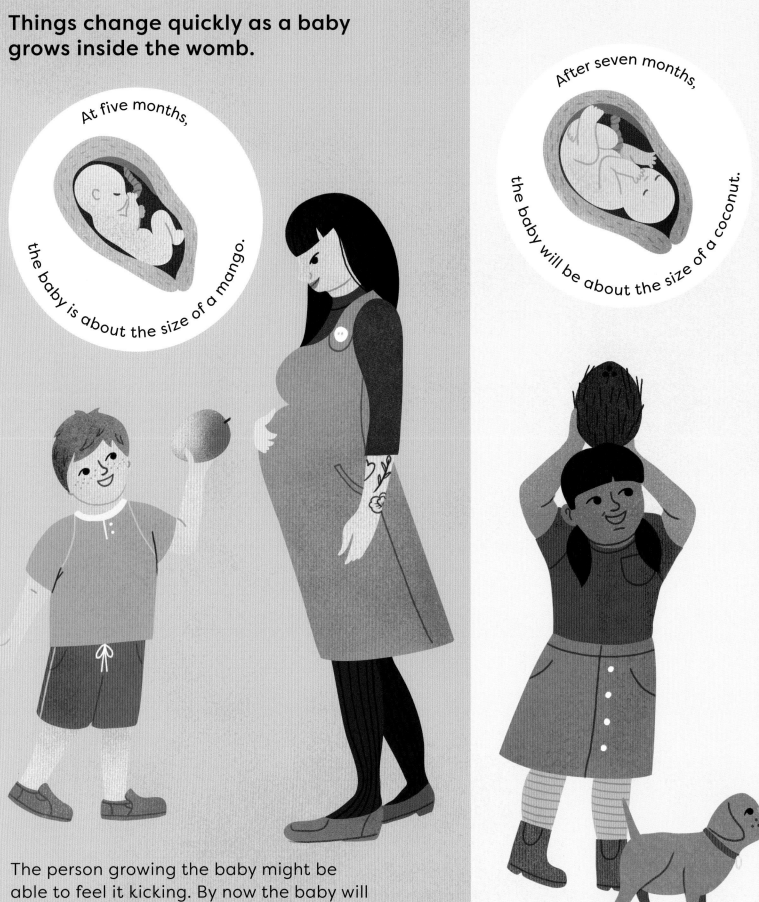

At five months, the baby is about the size of a mango.

After seven months, the baby will be about the size of a coconut.

The person growing the baby might be able to feel it kicking. By now the baby will be able to suck its thumb or fingers.

The baby can now open and close its eyes and tell the difference between light and dark. It has less room to wriggle around and *you* might be able to feel it kicking by touching the tummy of the person growing the baby.

At nine months, the baby is about the size of a medium pumpkin.

By now, most babies are ready to be born and are very squashed up inside the womb. They have moved so that their head is at the bottom of the womb, and now they spend all day upside down!

All of this has happened in just 40 weeks!

Sometimes two babies grow in one womb at the same time.

When one sperm and one egg meet, they make the very beginning of a baby.

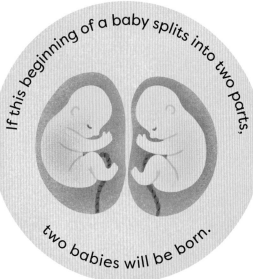

If this beginning of a baby splits into two parts, two babies will be born.

These babies' bodies and faces will look the same. They are called identical twins.

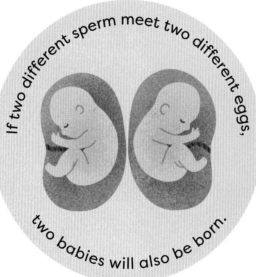

If two different sperm meet two different eggs, two babies will also be born.

These are called non-identical twins and don't always look like each other.

The most babies that have ever been grown together in one womb is eight. Imagine being born with seven siblings!

When it is time for a baby to come out of the womb, the person growing the baby will start to feel pains in their stomach and back.

This is when the muscles in the womb start to squeeze—which pushes the baby downward.

At the same time the opening of the womb, called the cervix, which was closed while the baby was growing, starts to open up. This is called labor because it's very hard work.

The squeezes get stronger and start to follow each other more and more quickly until it is time for the baby to be born. By this time, the cervix is as wide open as it can be.

When the person pushes hard at the same time as a really big squeeze, the baby is pushed down, through the vagina and into the world.

Welcome, baby!

**But not every baby is born in the same way.
A lot of babies are born by a special
operation instead.**

During the operation, in the hospital, the person
who grew the baby is given an injection, so they
won't feel any pain below the waist.

Next, a doctor cuts a small hole in the tummy
and womb, just big enough for the baby,
or babies, to get through.

The baby is born through this hole and brought into the world to meet its family.

The person who grew the baby has to have special stitches in their tummy to close the hole. Just like when you have cut your knee or your finger, after a few weeks, the hole heals up completely.

Within a few days, the person who grew the baby should be well enough to go home.

To make a baby you need one sperm,
one egg, and one womb . . .

. . . but every family starts
in its own special way.

You and your family are amazing,
just as you are!

Some extra questions you might have . . .

What is a person's sex?

When a baby is born, a doctor or a midwife looks to see whether the baby has a penis or a vulva. Babies who have penises are called boys (males). Babies who have vulvas are called girls (females). This is called their biological sex.

Some babies' bodies are a bit like a boy and a bit like a girl. These babies are intersex.

Some people grow up feeling that the biological sex they were given at birth is not their true sex, or that they don't belong to either sex. And some choose to make changes as they get older to help the way they look on the outside match up with the way they feel on the inside.

Why do some babies not grow?

Usually a baby takes nine months to grow in the womb. Sometimes, though, there is a problem that causes the baby to stop growing correctly, and after a few weeks or months, the baby will die. This is a very sad time for everyone who was excited about a new baby joining their family.

What happens when a baby is born too soon?

Sometimes babies arrive a few weeks, or even a few months, earlier than they are supposed to be born. When babies arrive very early, sometimes they need a bit of help from doctors and nurses to stay alive—because all of their important body parts haven't finished growing yet.

They might need to spend time in a special crib called an incubator and have help with their breathing and feeding until they are strong enough to come home.